A SIMPLE GU
PLANNING APPL_____

A SIMPLE GUIDE TO PLANNING APPLICATIONS

Second revised edition

Robert Cooke

Ian Henry Publications

© copyright, Robert Cooke, 1987, 1995

First published May, 1988
Reprinted, with corrections, October, 1988
2nd edition February, 1995

Cooke, Robert
A simple guide to planning applications.
1. England. Planning permission - Manuals
I. Title
711'.1

ISBN 0 86025 451 8

Printed by
Redwood Books
Kennet House, Kennet Way,
Trowbridge, Wiltshire BA14 8RN
for
Ian Henry Publications, Ltd.
20 Park Drive, Romford, Essex RM1 4LH

The author and the publishers would like to thank a number of Planning Officers for their help in bringing this new edition up to date.

The illustration on the cover is reproduced by kind permission of the Everett Partnership.

PLANNING CONTROL - WHY AND HOW

Suppose your next-door neighbour decided to start a small pig farm in his back garden, with pig pens where once the rose bed flourished. Or maybe you read in the local press of a scheme to build a bus garage on that very attractive site down the road and in the middle of your pleasant residential district. You and your neighbours might well regard such enterprises as an outrage, for the perfectly valid reason that they would be sadly out of keeping with the character and style of the surroundings and would result in loss of amenity for residents.

And that is what Planning Control is all about. It is a system to control the development and use of land and premises in the environmental interests of the community as a whole. Of course, like most regulatory controls, it has its weaknesses and it is sometimes difficult for ordinary mortals to understand the reasons behind planning control decisions. Nevertheless, it does not require much imagination to envisage what would happen without it. There are plenty of monstrosities created by developers before the advent of planning regulations and some of them will remain with us for years ahead.

The basis of planning control is that the consent of the planning authority must be obtained for any of a broad range of developments which can directly or indirectly affect the community and that members of the public shall have access to particulars of what is proposed, so that they may pursue objections to the proposals if they so wish.

Note that word DEVELOPMENT. It is a key word in planning matters and is defined in the *Town and Country Planning Act, 1990*, which is the statutory source of planning control. Section 55 of the Act says that, for purposes of planning control, DEVELOPMENT means the carrying out of building, engineering, mining or other operations in, on, over or under land, or by the making of any material change in the use of buildings or other land. And, although Section 55 goes on to list a number of things excluded from this general provision, its scope remains very wide indeed.

As far as the private dwelling holder is concerned, perspective can be provided by stating the types of situation where involvement with planning controls procedures is a

possibility, if not a probability. They are
> Building something, or altering an existing building
> Changing the use to which land or premises are put
> Objecting to some other person's plans to do any of these things.

Of course, there are plenty of activities coming under these headings which do not come within the scope of planning regulations, so you need to have a good idea of where the involvement starts. But, first of all, become familiar with the general structure and operation of planning control.

This is how it goes -

At the top of the tree is the Secretary of State for the Environment or the Secretary of State for Wales (depending on the location). He is the ultimate authority in town and country planning, but the odds are against your experience with planning control bringing you into direct contact with the dizzy heights of a Government Department. Most planning consent activity is completed at local level, where county and borough councils and sometimes district councils have planning departments staffed by professional planning officers and have the authority to approve most types of planning application. The decisions on applications are normally made by committees of elected councillors, advised by their planning officers and usually abiding by their advice, although it is not uncommon for planning committees to decide against their professional guidance.

The normal sequence of events in the progress of a planning application is:

i) An application is made on the prescribed forms to the local authority planning department

ii) The planning department acknowledges receiving the application and makes it known publicly that the application has been made. A copy of the application is kept in the offices for inspection by anyone who may wish to examine it

iii) Anyone wishing to object to the development proposed in the application can do so within a limited period of time

iv) After studying the application, considering its implications and taking note of any valid objections received, the planning department will prepare a report for the council committee, with recommendations on the decisions to be made and a note of the objections received

v) At one of its following meetings the committee will consider the application, together with the planning officer's report and recommendations, and will arrive at its own decisions, which will be communicated to the applicant by the planning department, along with any necessary comments or information
vi) If the applicant is not satisfied with the decisions or if there has been no notification of any decision within a certain period of time, an appeal can be made to the Secretary of State. There is more than one way in which the Minister can handle the appeal, but in any event his decision is final.

That is a simple outline of the procedure, which will be reviewed in more detail in later chapters.

As well as the normal considerations of planning control there are several possible circumstances of a general nature which can impose additional constraints on development. One or more of these may exist to affect a planning application you are making. Knowing the answers to the following questions is a prerequisite of seeking a planning consent.

Is a 'Listed Building' affected by the development?
Listed buildings are premises and structures (including walls and gateways) which have been listed by the Department of the Environment as being of special architectural or historical interest. Almost anything affecting the external appearance or structural design of such a building is likely to require what is known as Listed Building Consent, as well as other planning consent which may be needed.

Is the development within a Conservation Area?
Conservation areas are districts within much the same general criteria as listed buildings. They are defined by the local authority and are the subject of special restrictions and requirements designed to maintain standards of character and appearance. Here again the requirements are additional to normal planning consent. Similar requirements will apply in other types of conservation area, with such designations as 'Green Belt', 'Area of Outstanding Natural Beauty', 'National Park' or 'Site of Special Scientific Interest'.

Is an Article 4 Direction in force?
An 'Article 4 Direction' (the name derives from its source in Planning Law) is a set of restrictions which the local authority has applied to an area or even to a single building. The restrictions are often concerned with particular types of development for which planning consent is not normally required and they make it obligatory for prior consent to be obtained.

Is there a local development plan?
At some time or other most local planning authorities have published development plans, setting out policies and aims for future development in specified areas. They have the laudable objective of maintaining environmental standards and in some cases will include quite specific requirements, such as maximum number of dwellings per acre, minimum plot frontage, and so on. Some developers are inclined to regard these local plans merely as a form of wishful thinking and make determined efforts to circumvent their provisions, but the requirements are not set aside lightly when planning applications are under consideration. A planning application must be determined in accordance with the policies of the development plan, provided it is up to date and relevant, unless material considerations indicate otherwise. Moreover, it often happens that local development plans are stoutly defended by residents in the vicinity, with vigorous objections registered against any planning application attempting to contravene the objectives of a plan.

Is the property subject to a covenant?
In the context of property development, covenants are agreements between the original owners of the land and the persons who have acquired the land - or parts of it - for development purposes. As part of the covenant the buyers of the land are usually required to give an undertaking to abide by certain regulations or restrictions affecting future use of the land and the style of premises built on it. This sort of covenant often exists on housing estates developed since 1900. The constraints imposed in this way were intended as safeguards against lowered residential standards and include such things as limitations on the size of outbuildings, a ban on the

conversion of front gardens to 'hard standing' for vehicle parking and, sometimes, even a restriction on the range of permissable colours for exterior decoration of houses. There are residential property covenants made well over a century ago, but still binding on the owners of the property, because their terms require that continuation of covenant agreements is a condition of sale whenever there is change of ownership. Parts of many covenants have been overtaken by planning legislation introduced since the covenants were made and planning law usually takes precedence, but the fact of a covenant having been made a long time ago doesn't mean it can be ignored.

Is there existing planning permission?
Planning consent for some sort of development on a property may have been obtained by a previous owner and the time limitation for implementation may not have expired. It is just possible that discovery of such existing planning consent could save time and trouble in making a new and unnecessary application. It is also possible that an existing planning permission could create some sort of impediment to a new and different application.

For most buyers of property these questions will usually have been posed and answers obtained by their professional advisers - surveyors, solicitors - retained in connection with the purchase of the freehold or lease. Nevertheless, anyone contemplating a planning application should start clearing the decks for action by checking through them. The main source of information will be the local authority planning department, which will have all the facts you need, except, perhaps, those relating to covenants. As regards covenants, any existing on your property will be noted in the relevant Land Register entry.

Having read thus far, you may have decided that planning control law and procedures can be depressingly complex and confusing. And you will be right! In the local reference library you may find several feet of shelf space occupied by books on various aspects of the subject and you can give yourself a nasty shock by glancing through some of these tomes. That's the bad news.

The good news is that if your objective is no more than obtaining planning consent for sensible and non-vexatious development or, on the other side of the coin, to pursue a reasonable and well-founded objection to a development proposed by somebody else, there is a very good chance that you will get through the procedures without excessive hassle.

It is really just a matter of doing things the right way. Which is what this book is all about.

IS PLANNING PERMISSION NEEDED?

There is no comfortable formula to be applied in any given situation to determine whether or not planning permission is necessary. So in this chapter information is provided under a range of headings to cover the types of development in which a householder or flatholder may be interested. The observations are intended as general guide to the need - or otherwise - for planning application. In some cases it is possible to be specific about dividing lines, but all too often there are lots of 'ifs' and 'buts'. However, after reading this chapter, you should have a much clearer view of the subject, but whenever there is doubt don't hesitate to consult your local planning authority, for which we shall use the abbreviation 'LPA' in the many references made to it in the following pages.

In the previous chapter several special circumstances which may impose additional development restraints were mentioned. Before considering individual types of development there are two other general conditions to be noted. Irrespective of other aspects of a proposed development, planning consent must always be applied for if
a) there is any possibility that a safety hazard may be created by obstruction or limitation of the range of view on a vehicle highway, or
b) the development includes laying down a new vehicle or pedestrian outlet to a public thoroughfare, or enlarging an existing outlet.

Building New Premises
Plans for a new house or new premises of any kind require planning consent. For the private individual the most likely involvement with this class of development is in buying a plot of land as a building site, or buying land which already holds buildings to be demolished to make way for a new house. In these circumstances the buyer has - or should have - the benefit of professional advice. The solicitor acting for him in the legal aspects of buying the land (and presumably fully instructed as to his client's development intentions) will investigate such matters as the existence of constraints, such as covenants or existing planning consent with attached conditions. The architect or contractor employed to design the

new building will take planning control regulations and other relevant factors into account in preparing the design and will make the submission of necessary applications. Such professional support should be given without prompting, but any prudent person with money at risk will make sure of it. No solicitor will mind reassuring an anxious client and an architect or contractor should not object to being asked to confirm that the right things are being done.

One type of 'new house' development that often runs into stern opposition is where the building site was formerly part of the large garden of another house which is still standing. If, as is usually the case, the land is in a favoured and well-established residential area, 'infilling' of this sort may incur the wrath of other residents in the vicinity, well organised to resist unwanted developments and possibly enjoying the support of a Residents' Association or Civic Amenity Society. And, even though the proposed development may find no official objection, there can be much delay, bother and expense resulting from the local private opposition. A little advance checking on neighbourhood goodwill (or otherwise) might be worthwhile.

Repairs and Decoration

Repairs, maintenance work and decoration inside a building do not need planning consent. Nor does that class of work on the outside, provided that it does not make the building larger. But work on a 'Listed' building - especially work on the exterior - may need Listed Building Consent. External work may also need permission if the building is in a conservation area of any kind or within the scope of an estate covenant, Article 4 direction or anything in that category.

Extensions and Loft Conversions

It is reasonably safe to assume that planning permission is not needed for an extension to a house if the answer to each of the following questions is 'No'

i) Is the extension for use as a separate dwelling (for example, a self-contained flat)?

ii) Will the extension result in more than half of what was originally garden space being covered by buildings?

iii) Will any part of the extension coming within 2 metres of the

plot boundary be more than 4 metres above ground level?
iv) Will any part of the extension be higher than the original roof of the building?
v) Will any part of the extension be nearer to a public road or footpath or a service road than any part of the original building?
vi) Is the property listed?
vii) Will the volume of the original house (calculated on outside measurements) be increased beyond the following limits

a)*House in a terrace or in a conservation area (or in a National Park or an Area of Natural Beauty [AONB])* 50 cubic metres or 10% up to a maximum of 115 cubic metres, whichever is the greater;

b)*Other houses* - 70 cubic metres or 15% up to a maximum of 115 cubic metres, whichever is the greater.

In regard to i) above, **any** house extension designed or intended to be a separate dwelling, such as a flat or 'granny annexe', requires planning consent.

Another important point to note is the meaning of the words 'original' and 'originally', as used in planning regulations and as in ii), iv), v) and vi) above. They refer to the house as it was first built or as it was on 1st July, 1948, so it follows that any extensions made since that 1948 date will count towards the allowances.

Loft conversions are subject to similar considerations as other house extensions. Planning permission will be needed for any extension to the roof where it fronts a highway, and for increases in volume of over 40 cubic metres in the case of a terraced house, or 50 cubis metres in any other case. A key difference is that planning permission will be needed in conservation areas, national parks, an AONB or the Norfolk Broads.

As with building new premises, the likelihood is that professional services will be used with extensions and loft conversions and those services should include proper knowledge of and compliance with planning control requirements. But don't accept contractors' assurances too readily. Query anything that seems out of line with what you have just been reading.

Garages and Outbuildings

Most types of small outbuilding in the garden of a house will not require planning consent if associated with the residential amenities of the house and meet a few requirements as to position and size. Under this heading you can include garages, summer houses, swimming pools and enclosures, garden sheds, green houses, dog kennels, poultry pens, aviaries, and so on. The basic 'size and position' limitations to observe in making planning consent unnecessary are

the structure should not result in more than half of the original garden space being taken up by buildings (Note that the word 'original' has cropped up again)

no part of the structure should extend beyond the original house limits on any side facing a public road or footpath or a service road

the height should not exceed 3 metres (or 4 metres if it has a ridged roof).

the building has a volume in excess of 10 cubic metres and is within 5 metres of the house, including recent extensions.

Don't forget the definition given under the heading 'Extensions and Loft Conversions'.

Things will be different if the site is in a conservation area, a National Park, or a designated area of natural beauty. In those circumstances, the garage will always be regarded for planning control purposes as a house extension.

Conservatories and Sun Lounges

With the most popular arrangement of attachment to the side of the house, conservatories and sun lounges are treated as extensions. The same applies to enclosure of open verandahs. If, however, you want your conservatory or sun lounge separated from the house, you will need planning consent, unless you keep within the limits listed above for 'Outbuildings'.

Porches

To avoid the need for planning approval, keep your porch smaller than 3 square metres in ground area, 3 metres in overall height, and with at least 2 metres between it and any part of your garden's boundary with a public thoroughfare.

Roofs

Alterations to the roof of your house are unlikely to need planning consent if the height is not increased and there isn't a noticeable change in appearance. Altering the appearance of a roof can sometimes cause problems with what would otherwise be an acceptable development. For example, the cost of quite a modest side extension of a house could be increased considerably by the need to carry the pitched roof over the extension: there might be a temptation to economise by having a flat roof over the new part of the building. There would then be a possibility of the plan being turned down by the planners because of the effect on the appearance of the house elevation. So, if your plan for altering your roof increases its height or affects the appearance of the property in a way which might be considered detrimental, discuss the matter with the LPA before finalising.

Aerials, Satellite Dishes and Flagpoles

The popular practice of attaching a TV or radio aerial to the chimney or some other suitable part of a house does not need planning consent, but a rooftop aerial rising prominently above the highest point of the roof could be a contravention of an estate covenant or some other local regulation. A satellite dish will not require planning permission, but they normally have produced objections from local authorities and from neighbours in some localities: this is a particularly sensitive consideration in Conservation Areas. A preliminary enquiry of the LPA is recommended. Aerial masts and flagpoles set up in a garden are treated as outbuildings for planning purposes. This means that a mast or pole with a height of more than 3 metres from the ground must be the subject of a planning application.

External storage tanks

During the 1920s and 30s external catchment tanks for rainwater were a feature of many new houses, but nowadays the demand for a supply of soft, natural water seems to have abated.

However, if you are considering the addition of an external water tank to your property and especially if it is to be roof mounted, a prior word with the LPA is advisable. External oil storage tanks for central heating systems are free of planning control if their capacity does not exceed 3,500 litres, they are no higher than 3 metres from the ground and do not project beyond any part of the building which is facing a public thoroughfare. Bulk storage of petrol, diesel oil, chemicals and other liquids is covered by stringent controls and is generally out of the question on residential property.

Walls and Fences

The only specific planning restriction on a wall or fence is that its height shall be no more than 2 metres or no more than 1 metre if it is near a vehicle roadway or junction where a higher wall or fence might obscure a driver's view of oncoming traffic.

This is not to say that a planning application for a very high wall or fence is sure to be rejected. If there is a good reason for the height and no other person's valid interests are affected, it may receive approval.

Walls designated as listed buildings or within a conservation area are a different matter and may need Listed Building Consent for alterations, additions or removal.

Strangely, there are no specific or general planning restrictions on hedges, but you should not assume that this gives everyone *carte blanche* for unlimited hedge dimensions. There may be some local limitations to contend with.

Driveways, Pathways and Hard Standing

You must obtain planning consent for a driveway or footway giving access to a roadway, unless the roadway is unclassified and the drive or footway is related to some other development which does not need planning consent. The Highways or Engineering department of your local authority will tell you if a roadway is classified or unclassified. Chances of success with a planning application involving access to a classified roadway usually depend to a great extent on how much traffic the roadway carries. The busier the road, the greater the possibility of planning refusal.

The Highways or Engineering department will come into the matter again if a proposed vehicle access to a roadway will cross a pedestrian footway or roadside verge. Approval of the appropriate authority is an additional requirement to normal planning consent and it should be appreciated that vehicle access to a road carrying heavy traffic must be considered as a hazard.

Within the confines of your land, drives and pathways not giving direct access to a public thoroughfare will not need planning consent. The same applies to hard standing which you lay down in your garden and parking space for your car, caravan or boat and boat trailer. The situation could be different if you used the hard standing as a parking place for a vehicle used for trade (including taxicabs and hire cars). For example, if you parked a commercial delivery van (particularly one bearing the name and style of a business) regularly on your hard standing, it might be held that your land was being partly used for trade purposes. And this would come under the heading of 'Change of Use' (see below).

As always, don't forget to check on estate covenants, conservation area restrictions *et alia*. In some districts restrictions are imposed on large areas of hard standing in private house forecourts.

Caravans and Boats

Some local authorities have acquired special powers to prevent the parking of caravans and boats on the forecourts or front driveways of houses. A 'phone call to your LPA will establish the existence or otherwise of such a regulation. If there isn't such a restriction and you are doing no more than park your caravan or boat (and boat trailer) on your driveway or elsewhere in your garden when not in use, planning consent will not be needed. There is nothing to prevent you or your family making use of a caravan while it is standing on your land, but you must not make a separate dwelling of it. Nor should you use it for business purposes, such as office or storage accommodation. That could be regarded as business activity, requiring Change of Use planning consent.

Advertising Signs

You don't need permission to display small signs, such as election posters, notices of meetings, jumble sales, etc., on your property, but anything of a permanent or business nature may be within the scope of what is known as 'Advertisement Control'. You should check with your LPA, which can probably give you a free booklet or leaflet explaining in detail what does and what does not need approval. Fly-posting addicts who stick posters and other advertising matter on the windows of empty shops, walls, trees and other property should know that this practice is an offence under the Town & Country Planning Act, incurring (after prosecution and conviction) heavy fines.

Solar Panels

Solar energy panels are a fairly recent phenomena as far as private dwellings are concerned and they appear in a variety of shapes and sizes. The panels are often roof-mounted and, from the planning point of view, may affect the appearance of the premises. Contractors supplying and installing the equipment should be familiar with the attitude of the LPA to their installations and be able to advise, but you should certainly make planning consent a condition of any commitment to the contractor.

Demolition

You cannot knock down your house - or part of your house - without planning consent, if it is a listed building or is within a conservation area; you will also need the appropriate consent. When applying for permission you will need a very good reason for the demolition. There has to be valid justification, such as partial demolition being essential to the carrying out of beneficial restoration work.

Trees

Trees are so often the cause of friction between neighbours. Trees which are too tall, or overhang too much, are a source of too many falling leaves or have wandering roots with no respect for property boundaries, can cause powerful feelings. But such matters as these rarely fall within the meaning of planning regulations. With few exceptions, planning control is concerned only with trees protected by preservation orders or within a conservation area, but the control is strictly maintained.

If a tree on your land is the subject of a Tree Preservation Order (referred to in planning circles as a 'TPO'), your LPA will have a record of it and may carry out occasional checks to make sure it is still there and in good shape. There may also be unofficial surveillance by 'watchdog' conservation or civic interest groups. When a tree is protected by a TPO, prior permission must be obtained from the LPA to fell it, top it or lop it. All trees in a conservation area, whether or not they have TPOs, are protected. If you want to fell, top or lop[1] a conservation area tree, which has no TPO, you must give due notice of your intention to the LPA, thus giving that department time to check the need for the surgery. "It's my tree, on my land, so surely I can chop it down if I want to!" expresses a not uncommon attitude amongst householders, but it cuts no ice with the planners. Heavy fines can result from prosecutions arising from defiance of TPOs or conservation area regulations. Don't overlook the possibility that a TPO could have been placed on a tree on your land before you bought the land. Check it out!

Planning authorities are not immovable in the resistance to the felling of protected trees and will give all due consideration to reasonable arguments put forward by applicants for permission to fell. For instance, if the removal of a tree was essential to an approved building development, felling permission might be given with a proviso that a replacement tree should be planted in a suitable position nearby. But there must always be a good reason for felling.

Change of Use and Business Use
Under this heading we are concerned with:

Changes in the trade or profession carried on in established business premises;

Introduction of business activity to a residential dwelling;

Conversion of residential premises into business premises;

Conversion of business premises into residential accommodation.

Although it may transpire in a few odd instances that planning consent is not necessary it should be taken as a general rule that planning applications should be submitted for

---

1 'Lopping' is normally defined as any cutting which requires more than the use of small hand secateurs.

any development in these groups. The range of possible circumstances is infinite, but in considering applications the planning authority will certainly have the following three main factors in mind

The extent - existing and potential - of the business activity

The effect of the business activities on the neighbourhood and the people who live and/or work in that area

The existing or future planned character of the neighbourhood.

To illustrate how these factors may be applied, let us take some examples. Consider a situation where a person wants to run a business from his home. If it is an 'invisible' operation, requiring only (say) the use of a desk, typewriter and telephone, and creating no effects noticeable to other residents nearby, there is not likely to be any difficulty in obtaining planning consent, even though the premises are in a quiet residential district. But suppose that business - although still requiring no more in the way of office equipment - was some sort of employment or appointments bureau which might result in a noticeable number of people calling at the house, perhaps loitering in the vicinity and maybe causing car parking problems and roadway obstructions. This could be regarded as something of a nuisance in a residential area, there would probably be strong objections from neighbours, and planning consent might well be withheld. If, on the other hand, the location was in a fairly busy road with other businesses, as well as residential property, there would be a better chance of obtaining consent.

The provision of living accommodation is a popular form of home business enterprise which many people believe - quite innocently, but none the less mistakenly - to have no relevance to planning regulations. The range of possible activity in the home extends from a single 'lodger', living as a member of the family, up to the conversion of part of the house into self-contained flats. Although taking in one or two 'paying guests' is not likely to be regarded as a change of use requiring planning consent, a planning application will probably be needed for anything going beyond that

Letting 'bed-sitters' will require an application, but should be successful unless some palpably adverse effect on the neighbourhood is thought to be a possibility.

Conversion of a house or part of a house into self-contained flats will always need planning consent, but if it is sensibly planned, has no undesirable effect on the building exterior and will not create any loss of residential amenity in the immediate vicinity, there should not be any difficulty in obtaining planning approval.

Situations often arise in which business is introduced to residential property to a minor extent without planning consent and the offender is disagreeably surprised when the planning authority - prompted by complaints from neighbours - takes an interest in matters. A typical example of this is where someone who runs a business at premises away from home makes obvious use of part of his house in connection with the business. This could include such activities as using the garage as storage for business stock or regularly parking trade vehicles in the front driveway overnight.

It isn't clever to put off making a planning application until other residents complain. Far better to do things properly. If there is nothing really objectionable about what you want to do, planning permission will usually be given.

MAKING A PLANNING APPLICATION

You may be in the happy position of being able to employ an architect or other professional assistance in a proposed development, in which case the hired help will be looking after the matter of the planning application. Many of the building firms specialising in extensions also include planning applications in their services. When someone else submits a planning application on your behalf that person is acting as your agent and any communications from the LPA will be addressed to that agent. But you will be named on the application as the actual applicant.

You don't have to be the owner of the land in order to make a planning application, but the application must disclose your interest in the property.

If, for example, you are contemplating the purchase of a plot of land on which to build a house and you want to make sure of planning consent before committing yourself to buy, your interest will be that of 'prospective purchaser'. But the Planning Act does insist that owners of land are properly informed of any planning applications made by non-owners.

All the forms needed for a planning application are available from the LPA. If possible you should call to collect them personally, so that, at the same time, you can have a brief discussion on your intended development with a planning officer. Most LPAs welcome this sort of preliminary discussion, which often saves both sides a lot of wasted time and trouble.

PLANS AND DRAWINGS

Plans and drawings are an essential feature of planning applications. On major developments where architects or other professional aides are used production of these drawings will be part of the service and the same will apply when builders are employed for house extensions and so on. The plans and drawings associated with an application are -

SITE PLAN. To indicate the location of the development site in relation to adjacent properties and nearby public roads. It must be capable of identification in relation to the Ordnance Survey for the district. The minimum scale is 1:2500 (or 1:1250 if the site is in a built up area) and the land to which the application refers should be outlined in red. If the applicant owns or has control of any adjacent land, that should be outlined in blue.

BLOCK PLAN. Required when the application refers to the construction or structural alteration of a building or buildings to show the layout plan of the site with all existing and proposed buildings, trees and other natural features, existing and proposed access ways, existing and proposed drainage arrangements and a lot of other information. A scale of not less than 1:500 is required.

BUILDING PLANS. Detailed drawings (*i.e.* plans, elevations and cross-sections) of proposed new buildings or alterations to existing buildings. The drawings must carry full information in such things as the materials to be used, exterior colours and textures, etc. If measurements are metric the minimum scale is 1:100, modified to 1:96 if dimensioned in feet.

A householder who finds himself saddled with the task of providing these plans and drawings can take comfort from the fact that, as far as his existing house is concerned, there will be a site plan and, probably, a block plan attached to the conveyance documents in his or his solicitor's safe keeping.

The detailed drawings for an extension or alteration to an existing house are not something to be considered lightly. If it is a 'standard' extension or garage unit to be provided by a builder or in a 'kit' form for erection by the householder, the necessary drawings will almost certainly be available from the builder or supplier. A possible alternative is to obtain the services of a freelance draughtsman to convert the householder's ideas into acceptable drawings. Or the householder may prefer to tackle the job himself if he can produce a clear, accurate drawing. LPAs do not insist on the highest standards of draughtsmanship, but they do need properly detailed intelligible drawings. Original drawings should be in ink. Photocopies or copies produced by other reprographic processes must be clear and free of reproduction blemishes which may obscure detail. Original drawings and reproductions ought to be on good, durable paper - not on material which starts to fall to pieces after a few foldings and unfoldings.

TYPES OF PLANNING APPLICATION

What sort of planning application do you need to make? It will come under one of the following headings.

OUTLINE. Put in an application for 'Outline' consent when you want to put up a building or buildings and wish to know that the development will be approved, subject to the details of the buildings being satisfactory. This is a useful type of application, but it will be necessary to obtain approval of the details before building work starts. The application does not need to be supported by a block plan or a detailed building plan. In fact, you need not have decided on the details when you make the application. You can submit the details at this stage, should you wish, and can do so on the understanding that they may be changed when it comes to a final stage of planning consent. Even if you are not submitting detailed drawings with the outline application you will need to give a general idea of the building or buildings you have in mind. If you are not sufficiently informative the LPA may ask for more particulars before they consider the application.

RESERVED MATTERS. This is the essential follow-up to an Outline application which has been approved and is a submission of the details not disclosed previously.

FULL PLANNING PERMISSION. This is the most widely used type of planning application and is made in respect of the erection or alteration of buildings or a change in the use of land or buildings. There are no preliminary or 'outline' stages.

RENEWAL OF LIMITED PERMISSION. When planning consent has been given for a development, but only for a limited period of time, an application can be made for the time to be extended for a further period. Similarly, if planning consent was given for, say, a use of land or premises provided that certain requirements or conditions were observed, application can be made for permission to continue the use for a period without complying with the special conditions. This sort of application is seldom needed by a private householder, but naturally there are exceptions.

CERTIFICATE OF LAWFUL USE OR DEVELOPMENT (CLEUD). A CLUED can be applied for to formally regularise a use of land or buildings which has never received planning consent, but has nevertheless continued for at least ten years. It can also be applied for if you wish to know whether or not a proposed development comes within the meaning of the Planning Act as requiring planning consent, there being some doubt in the matter. The response of the planning authority will not go beyond a determination and will hold no indication of the possible success or otherwise of an application.

LISTED BUILDING CONSENT. Although this is a separate matter from the normal planning procedure, an application for LBC can be combined with a planning application, using a separate form.

THE FORMS

The principal form used for planning applications for listed building consent and conservation area consent is a two-page (or double sided single sheet) questionnaire. They vary in layout depending on the Local Planning Authority, but each includes the following requirements:

Particulars of applicants and (if any) Agent.

Type of Application. Space is provided for an indication that Listed Building Consent is also required.

Address of Land or Buildings to which application relates.

Applicant's interest. It must be stated if the applicant is the freeholder, leaseholder or tenant of the site or, if none of these, the indirect interest (such as prospective purchaser). Any ownership or control of adjacent land must also be declared.

Description of proposed development. Although very little space is provided on the form, a very complete description is required. It is better to put this on a separate sheet of paper and draw attention to it on the form.

Fees [see explanation of fees later in this chapter].

Access to site and Parking. The section is concerned with confirmation of any vehicle or pedestrian access provisions or changes, new road or footpath constructions, and other similar features which will, of course, be shown on the accompanying plans.

Other details of development. Here, again, confirmation is required of details shown on accompanying plans - site areas, drainage lines, building materials and so on. If the development work entails felling trees, it should be mentioned in this section.

Previous use of land or buildings. A brief statement of previous usage is required. If the site is vacant the last known use can be stated.

Signature (of applicant or agent) and date.

Certification of Ownership or Notice to Ownership. This final section is related to the requirement for owners (and, in some cases, tenants) of land to be given proper notice of any planning applications made by others in respect of the land. Certification is required by the applicant or his agent that he is either the sole owner of the land or, if not, that due notice of the application has been given for the benefit of the owners. If any part of the land is agricultural and is tenanted, it must also be certified that notice has been provided for the tenants. There are several ways of giving notice, described later in this chapter.

With an application for outline planning permission, answers need not be given to many of the questions of detail, unless specifically requested by the LPA. In applications for approval of 'reserved matters', part of the form is used to state which details are now being submitted for approval, and it must be kept well in mind that the application will not be valid if any of the details cannot be associated with the outline approval already given. When outline approval is given, a deadline of not longer than three years is set for putting in the necessary reserved matters application. If the deadline is exceeded the outline permission lapses.

The form is also used for explaining what relief is being sought in applications for renewal of time limited conditions or removal of conditions applied by the LPA to previous planning approval. The date and reference or the original approval should be stated.

Four copies of the form, separately signed, are required by the LPA. Four copies of all plans and drawings should be attached. No plans are needed in support of applications for renewal of limited permission or relief from special conditions.

If a planning application refers to business use, the application form may be supplemented by another form, sometimes known as 'Part 2', covering industrial, office, warehousing, storage and retailing. This can include such details as

1. (Applicable to industrial developments) A description of the processes and machinery to be installed.
2. (Applicable where the application refers to a stage of a larger scheme for which permission is not yet sought in full) Advance information, if available, on what is envisaged in the main scheme.
3. Relationship of any proposed development to any existing use on or near the site.

4. (Applicable where the development is a replacement of existing premises elsewhere) Details of premises being replaced and a statement of intentions in respect of them.
5. Floorspace measurements (metric).
6. Numbers and classifications of employees involved.
7. Vehicle loading/unloading and parking arrangements.
8. Estimate of frequencies of vehicle attendances at site.
9. Particulars of disposal of trade effluents, if any.
10 Particulars of storage of hazardous materials, if any.
11 Signature (or applicant or agent) and date.
This form is also required in quadruplicate.

Applicationbs for listed building and conservation area consent or press advertisement consent, and certificates of lawful use and develeopment are made on separate forms.

INFORMING OWNERS
Section 65 of the Planning Act insists that an LPA cannot give consideration to any planning application not covered by the applicant's certification that the owners (and, where applicable, the tenants of agricultural land forming the whole or part of the site have been given notice of the application. For the purpose of this requirement 'Owner' means the freeholder or the holder of a lease having an unexpired period of seven years or more.

Obviously there is no requirement for owner notification when the applicant is the sole owner of the land, but if the applicant is only a part owner or has no ownership interest or there are agricultural tenants involved, there is an obligation for notification.

If the identity of all the owners is known, written notice with the following wording should be served on each of them:

TOWN & COUNTRY PLANNING GENERAL DEVELOPMENT ORDER, 1988
NOTICE UNDER ARTICLE 12 OF APPLICATION FOR PLANNING PERMISSION
Proposed development at ..... I give notice that ..... is applying to the ..... Council for planning permission to .....
Any owner of the land or tenant who wishes to make representations about this application should write to the Council at ....
Signature [applicant or agent]

On behalf of [applicant's name if notice served by agent]
Date:

If the site address as stated in the notice does not adequately locate the position of the site, it is advisable to attach a copy of the site plan to each notice served.

The certificate that notice has been given to owners in this way is included in the planning application form and it should be noted that the wording states that the requisite notice was given to all persons who were owners 20 days before the date of the planning application.

Where agricultural tenants are concerned and their identities are known, they should be served with the same notification, and this action is also certified in the planning application form.

If the identity of some, but not all, of the owners is known, the form of notification, as above, is to be served on each of those identified. For the benefit of owners not known to the applicant a notice must be published in a local newspaper not earlier than 21 days before the date of the planning application. The required wording of the newspaper notice is the same.

A copy of the published notice must be sent to the LPA, giving the name of the newspaper and the date of publication. If you have carried out the combination procedure of individually served notices and newspaper annoiuncement yoou will need to complete Certificate C (obtainable from the LPA) and submit it with the planning application.

In the event that the identity of none of the owners can be established by the applicant the published newspaper announcement is used in the same way as described above. This action is to be confirmed on Certificate D, obtained from the LPA and submitted with the application.

The responsibility for displaying a notice of the planning application on the actual site is often accepted by the LPA, but there may be instances where the onus is upon the applicant. This point should be cleared with the LPA at an early stage.

APPLICATION FEES
Fees for the processing of planning applications were introduced in 1981. A few types of application escape the charges, but there are lengthy and detailed regulations covering the basis of fee calculation, the grounds for fee remission, etc.

It is not intended to go into all the minutiæ of fee regulations in this small book, but the following broad summary of fee rates (current at the time of going to press, but subject to possible revision if new regulations are issued) will provide a guide to the charges for the more popular types of application. There is a discussion document currently being considered by which LPAs might have their own individual scales of fees.

Type of application	Basis of fee calculation
Listed Building Consent	No fee
Alterations or extensions to existing houses or flats	For one house or flat - £80 For 2 or more houses or flats - £160
Erection of new houses or flats	Outline approval - £160 for each 0.1 hectare (or part) of site area, to a maximum of £4,000. Full planning permission or approval of reserved matters - £160 for each house or flat to be created, to a maximum of £7,000
Change of use of existing dwelling to more houses or flats	£140 for each additional dwelling created, to a maximum of £8,000
Change of use of any building to 1 or more houses or flats	£160 for each dwelling created to a maximum of £8,000
Other changes of use not covered above	£160

Fees may be waived in some circumstances. For example, no fee is payable if the sole object of a proposed alteration or extension of a dwelling is to provide more comfort or mobility for a disabled person or if an application is a revision of an earlier application made within the previous 12 months and refused by the LPA. The private householder is unlikely to become involved with the sort of planning application requiring a large fee and can safely accept the LPA's assessment of the correct charge. Much time can be wasted in disputes over small differences in application fees. Where there is a dispute extending beyond a period of eight weeks, the applicant is entitled to appeal to the Secretary of State on the grounds that, in effect, the LPA has turned down his application. The government department is then drawn into the argument as to whether or not the correct fee has been charged. Unless a substantial sum of money is at stake this would seem to be a situation to be avoided.

The golden rule, therefore, is to make sure of the correct fee amount and enclose it with the application.

RECEIVING THE DECISION

Provided that everything is in order the LPA should respond to the receipt of an application within a matter of days by sending a formal acknowledgement. Two important things on that acknowledgement are the LPA's reference number (to be quoted in all subsequent communications) and the date (from which the period of time allowed for processing the application starts). If there is some irregularity in the application the response may be a note to that effect. If this should happen a personal visit to the LPA to put things right is recommended as a means of minimising delay.

When the decision on the application arrives it will not necessarily be a plain 'yes' or 'no'. From the applicant's point of view, complete and unqualified approval of the development proposal is the best result. At the other end of the scale is a complete rejection of the proposal. And, in between, are various stages of partial or conditional approval, carrying any of a wide range of limitations and requirements. All refusals, limitations and special conditions will be explained fully, together with the reasons behind them.

Even with the most disappointing decision on an application, all may not be lost. This is the time to take advantage of the advisory service which LPAs provide.

The applicant should make an appointment to see the planning officer concerned with his application and seek his advice as to the possibility of changes in the proposal which would make it acceptable. This sort of advice is invaluable and is given readily by LPA staffs.

Very little, if anything, is likely to be gained by storming into the LPA office and adopting an aggressive stance. Planning officers are not always right in their judgement, but you can be sure that they have considered an application fairly on the basic principle that a development should not be obstructed unless there is a valid planning reason for rejecting it or for requiring changes to it. Only by understanding such a reason is there any hope of finding an acceptable alternative.

If, after a thorough discussion with the LPA, an applicant retains a strong feeling that the refusal or qualifying requirements are wrongly based, he can start thinking about an appeal.

And that's another chapter!

OBJECTIONS

When a planning application is received by a planning authority, the authority takes steps to provide reasonable notice to the public that an application has been made and that the particulars can be seen on request at the LPA .

The media used for this purpose normally includes a notice posted on or adjacent to the site of the proposed development and lists of planning applications (usually made up weekly) placed in public libraries or displayed on notice boards outside the local authority premises. Some planning authorities send individual notifications to occupiers of premises near the development site, but this type of warning should not be relied upon as LPAs have no legal requirement to do this. If you wish to be on the alert for proposed developments that may affect you, find out which notification medium is convenient for you to check on and establish a scrutiny routine for yourself.

Should any notified application attract your attention you can discover the essential details by calling at the LPA, quoting the reference number given on the notification and asking to see the application. Most LPAs provide tables and seats so that you can settle down to a careful study of the development proposals. You should have a notebook with you to jot down the salient points instead of trusting to memory. The notes will be helpful if you wish to prepare an objection to the application.

Having seen the application you may be reassured that there is nothing for you to worry about, but if you are not used to technical descriptions and drawings and have a feeling that you have not fully understood what is being proposed, do not hesitate to ask to speak to a planning officer. You may have to wait a few minutes before this personal attention becomes available, but advice and explanations are always given willingly.

Don't delay in making this visit to the LPA to check on an application. Time is not on your side. In most casesthere is no more than 21 days time allowance (counting from the date of the notification) for objections to be prepared and submitted, and there is much to be done.

If and when you feel strongly enough about a planning application to put in a formal objection, start by getting the basis of your objection clear in your own mind. All objections have to be in writing - this might seem obvious to you, but it is surprising how many people believe that an objection can take the form of one irate telephone call of protest to the planning authority. So your first action should be to write down your objection and then read it through, critically, two or three times. Far too many objectors waste time with emotive statements stemming rather obviously from selfish personal considerations, having little or no relevance to the general community interests. This is not to say that it is wrong for an objector to draw attention to the possibility of his being put at a disadvantage by a proposed development, even if he and his family are the only persons who may be affected adversely, always provided that the complaint is based on a genuine loss of amenity that a resident should not reasonably be expected to suffer. Of course, an objector will be on stronger ground if it can be shown that more than one household or group will be disadvantaged.

GETTING SUPPORT

Having considered all this carefully and feeling assured that there is a proper basis for objection, get down to the task of invoking the interest and support of others. You may find neighbours who are already aware of the planning application in question and who are ready to join in a protest. You may also find a disturbingly large number who are unaware - or only vaguely aware - of what is afoot and you must be prepared to explain matters to them in order to enlist their support and that of your local Councillors. If there is a Residents' or Tenants' Association or a Civics Interest group in your area, that should be a prime contact. An active group ought to be aware of all planning applications with possible implications for the community or area of its concern, but you might have to do some alerting.

When you have determined the extent of the support for an objection, make sure everyone is involved in the action. Go over the grounds of the objection with everybody. It is quite possible that one or two people will come up with additional arguments. Make use of the good suggestions and resist those which you know will be a waste of time.

In rallying your support you will have to fight that old

enemy - apathy. Only half-believe well-meaning people who tell you they will 'write a letter'. They really think it themselves at the time, but rarely get around to doing it. Something has to be put in front of them to sign and the easiest way is to organise a petition, although it should be emphasised that letters from individuals normally carry more credence than a petition, which some Committee Members might regard as being signed simply to get you off the doorstep!

STATING THE CASE
The golden rule for the text of a petition or a letter of objection is to keep it short and sweet. And that means using plain language to make straightforward points without unnecessary embroidery. Avoid being emotional and never use a belligerent or sarcastic style. Planning officers are interested in valid arguments and relevant information, but are not impressed by threat of further action if the application is approved.

Construct the letter or petition on orderly lines. Address the senior officer of the planning authority by title - not by name. The title may be 'Director of Planning', 'Senior Planning Officer' or some other variation on that theme: although it won't be a catastrophe if you don't get it right, it doesn't add weight if you start off with a mistake. Head the text with the planning application reference number and short description, as used by the planning authority in its notification. Then get down to business with an opening sentence that states the intention.

Please note our/my objection to the above planning application, the grounds of the objection being...

Your reasons for objecting should follow. If there are several points to be made, make them in separate numbered paragraphs. Having made the points, conclude by asking that they are taken into account when the application is considered and add a request to be informed of the decision. Some Councils will allow objectors to speak at their Committee meetings and all will allow the opublic to attend their meetings. Most planning authorities do tell objectors of their decisions as a matter of course, but it doesn't do any harm to ask.

There is no avenue of appeal for an objector when the objection fails to achieve the desired result.

People sometimes shrink from objecting to a planning application, fearing that the applicant will find out and may take offence. Whether or not to object and the possible consequences of social friction which might result are matters for individuals to decide upon for themselves, but where there are valid grounds for objection it could be borne in mind that the applicant has not been deterred by consideration for the interests of other people and should not feel resentment if others are exercising their right to take defensive action.

Should the planning application be rejected or given only qualified approval which satisfies their objections, the objectors are entitled to feel that they have been successful in their battle. But they may not have won the war, because the applicant may decide to appeal. Determined objectors will then have to mobilise again, although now they will have the encouragement of knowing that the LPA is on their side.

VIGILANCE IS NEEDED
If you believe that vigilance in matters of planning control affecting the community is an important contribution to civic interest, it is worth bearing in mind that the scope for such vigilance is not restricted to the scrutiny of new planning consent applications. Offenses against planning regulations are happening all the time at many business premises in the form of unauthorised changes of use. A lot of these abuses are unfavourable to the community interest, because if unchecked they may become the thin ends of undesirable wedges.

Business premises used in excess of the limitations on their planning approval are all too common. A typical example is a building or part of a building carrying planning approval for storage only, but which is not infrequently used for such things as the repair of delivery vehicles used in the business, or for a partial or complete manufacturing process.

The first action to take when suspect activities are noted is to make sure of the scope of the planning approval already given to the use of the premises. The LPA will provide you with this information, which is a matter of public interest and in no way confidential. If your suspicions are confirmed, report the matter to the senior enforcement officer at the LPA. It may be that when the offenders are questioned they will offer a denial or some explanation, but they will realise that they have been rumbled and will think more than twice about repeating the offence. So you will have achieved the real object of the exercise.

When you have made a complaint to an enforcement officer he will normally report back to you after his investigation. If you don't hear from him after a reasonable time, follow the matter up.

Another example of misuse of business premises is when an unacceptable proportion of the working activities spill out of the premises on to the footpath and roadway. Obstruction of the footpath is, of course, a police matter and could even come within the scope of the Environmental Health Department or the Health & Safety at Work Inspectorate, but there is also an important question of planning control arising from frequent loading and unloading of commercial vehicles in the roadway and occupying a considerable area of public thoroughfare. In a locality where there are residential properties this over-spill of business activity could be adjudged a significant loss of residential amenity. There might be divergence of opinion on this, but it can be pointed out that the form for planning applications involving business premises does require a statement of estimated vehicle attendances. An investigation might reveal a very considerable disparity between the original forecast and what actually happens.

Taking an active interest in preventing or reducing abuses of planning regulations - unless carried out to an excess of zeal - should not be regarded as a busybody occupation. It can and does serve a useful purpose. After all, the LPA enforcement officers can't keep a watchful eye on everything. They need help.

APPEALS

The two basic situations in which a frustrated applicant for planning approval can appeal to the Secretary of State for the Environment (or the Secretary of State for Wales) are

i) The LPA has failed to give a decision on the application within eight weeks of the date when it acknowledged receiving it (or within any longer period which has been agreed), and

ii) The LPA has given a decision which is either a complete or partial refusal of the proposed development or has given approval subject to certain conditions or limitations.

In effect, an appeal in situation i) will be asking the Minister to take over the matter and give a decision. In ii) the appeal will ask for a reconsideration of all or part of what has been rejected or of all or part of conditions or limitations imposed, but the Minister's representative dealing with the appeal may decide that it is necessary to reconsider other parts of the LPA decision.

It must be appreciated that entering into an appeal is getting into much deeper water than might have been contemplated when the planning application was first made. Appeals can be costly and discouraging affairs, particularly when they are too hasty and ill-considered. Certainly there should be careful and patient discussions with the LPA before breaking off negotiations at that level.

Consider these facts

Records show that the odds are against a successful appeal and many appeals are withdrawn by their sadder and wiser instigators before they have run their course.

With few exceptions an appeal is presented most effectively with professional guidance and assistance. This sort of aid is expensive, unless the appellant is lucky enough to find some organisation willing to provide it on a voluntary basis.

While it is not essential for an appellant to have professional representation, paddling his own canoe will mean a heavy personal commitment to considerable work entailed by the preparation and presentation of the appeal and maintaining observance of the strict time schedule of the official procedure.

It could be as long as nine months from the time when the appeal is registered until the appeal decision. At best, it is unlikely to be less than five months. The possibility that such delays could have economic consequences in respect of a proposed development should not be overlooked.

Having said all that, it is nevertheless the right of a planning applicant to use the appeal procedure to seek what he feels should be planning control justice. It is unfortunate that a major factor in the decision to appeal or not to appeal will be the economic considerations. A person with ample financial resources may be more inclined to go ahead than someone who can ill afford the time and expense.

FIRST STEP

Whatever the financial status of the would-be appellant, the first action to be taken should be to seek an informed evaluation of the strength of the grounds for appeal. He would be best advised to go to a professional adviser, such as an independent planning consultant - preferably with local knowledge and experience. If there is a real need to limit expense it may be possible to obtain the backing of a voluntary organisation providing a planning advisory service without charge or at low cost. The nearest Residents' Association may know of such an organisation or the Citizens' Advice Bureau - although most unlikely to be able to offer direct aid - will know of any voluntary service available.

It is essential that whoever is making this important preliminary appraisal is given all the information available; not only documentary, but also verbal comments, observations and suggestions made by LPA planning officers at meetings with them. It is also essential that the prospective appellant receives a 'warts and all' assessment of the strengths and weaknesses of the appeal case as a basis for the decision on whether or not to take matters further.

Quite reasonably, voluntary organisations offering help to private individuals in planning problems are unlikely to extend their support beyond an initial consultation unless convinced that the appeal would be in the interests of righting a genuine wrong. They cannot be expected to waste their resources on an appeal which flies in the face of planning regulations or has no relevance to upholding community or individual rights. If this sort of negative response is forthcoming it is a strong indication that the chances of success are very small - or nil!

In such a situation or on getting an unencouraging opinion from a private professional adviser, the appellant will probably do well to forget the appeal and go back to the LPA to seek some kind of acceptable compromise. When taking this latter course he may be agreeably surprised to find that, although accorded a reception not quite up to the prodigal son standard, he receives a sympathetic and helpful hearing.

APPEAL PROCEDURES

Before an appeal is formally entered the appellant must decide on which appeal procedure is preferable. He can choose either of the following

Written procedure. The appeal will be decided without personal attendance of any of the parties concerned, but with 'written evidence' (including drawings, plans and photographs, as well as statements).

Local Inquiry. This is a hearing held at premises within the local authority area concerned, with verbal as well as documentary evidence given for the appellant and the LPA, and for other interested parties who may decide to intervene.

In both procedures the appeal is presided over by an Inspector appointed by the Secretary of State and empowered either to give a decision in his own right or to report, with recommendations as to a decision, to the Minister.

The choice of procedure is not entirely a matter for the applicant. Although he may have decided in favour of the written procedure the LPA or the Ministry may insist on a local inquiry. Usually they are in favour of the written procedure, which saves time and money, but a local inquiry is sometimes deemed necessary when there is public interest in the development or the evidence is complicated.

There is a possible third alternative form of procedure which may be suggested by the Ministry when the applicant has asked for the written procedure, but the LPA requires a local inquiry. This alternative is an 'informal hearing', at which the submissions and evidence, presented in written form, will be discussed on an informal basis by the parties concerned, under the control of the Inspector appointed.

Most appellants opt for the written procedure and the great majority of planning appeals are dealt with in this way. The cost of professional assistance in preparing the 'written' appeal will be considerably less than representation at a local inquiry. The advantage of a local inquiry is that witnesses can be questioned, evidence can be challenged and there is the opportunity to address the presiding Inspector personally. For the appellant presenting his own case and without the ability to 'think quickly on his feet', however, these advantages may prove to be something of an ordeal.

STRUCTURE OF APPEAL

An appeal must be lodged within six months of the date of the LPA's decision on the original application or, in the case of non-determination, within 6 months of the expiry of the 8 week period. At the same time the appellant must state his preference of appeal procedure. Irrespective of which procedure is chosen, the appeal statement must be a full account of the grounds of the appeal, supported by relevant plans, drawings and other documents. the central document of the appeal statement is the official planning appeal form, obtained from the Planning Inspectorate, Bristol, or the Welsh Office, Cardiff. But before starting the task of compiling the appeal statement, it is essential to have the format of the appeal case clearly in mind. There are two positions which can he taken up -

    a) disagreement with the reasons given by the LPA for rejecting the application or requiring certain conditions, or

    b) claiming that, even if the reasons have merit, they do not outweigh other considerations in favour of the development.

With a) the validity of the reasons must be challenged on grounds of disputed facts or disputed judgment, or both, and with b) it will be necessary to have convincing arguments and evidence that the development would have sufficient advantages to over-ride the LPA objections or conditions. It is quite reasonable to put forward b) in addition to a). the second line of appeal will not be prejudiced by the failure of the first.

No matter what the structure of the appeal case it is vitally important for the appeal statement to contain every available item of information. The relevance of each supporting document and illustration (drawings, sketches, photographs, copies of other documents, maps, etc.) should be made clear. If each item in the document 'bundle' is given a reference number or letter it becomes easier to associate it with the appeal statement.

In the same way that owners and agricultural tenants of the development land were to be notified of the original planning application, notification is again required in respect of the appeal. As previously, a certificate that this obligation has been met (or is unnecessary) is to be submitted with the appeal statement. This and other components of the appeal procedure are explained in notes sent out with the appeal form.

DON'T BE A LONER

Appellants with the benefit of professional assistance will not have to be involved with the details of appeal statement preparation, although they will have need to liaise closely with the consultant retained. For the private individual brave enough to face up to the job on his own, the best advice is to abandon the 'loner' rôle and to find someone who can be of genuine help - on the good old principle that two heads are better than one. If assistance is forthcoming from someone with actual knowledge or experience of planning matters it will be a boon. Failing that, a friend whose working occupation or other experience includes the preparation of formal reports, has legal or property development experience or - even without such a background - is intelligent and literate can be a tremendous help. Objective thinking becomes easier when there is someone to act as Devil's Advocate or to provide the other half of a constructive discussion.

'WRITTEN' INQUIRY

When the written procedure is to be used a copy of the appeal form must be sent to the LPA with copies of any documents it has not seen previously at the same time that the appeal is submitted to the Ministry. The latter will acknowledge receipt, giving a 'starting date' and reference number. The Ministry will send a copy of this acknowledgment to the LPA, which must then compile a statement of its own case by completing a questionnaire, backed by copies of relevant documents, and information as to other interested parties. The appellant receives this statement of the LPA case and can make observations on the contents. It is not obligatory to offer observations and it will not be advantageous to do so unless it adds weight to the appeal.

The Inspector dealing with the appeal will be inspecting the site of the proposed development on his own. The date of the inspection will be notified to the appellant and he can attend at the same time if he so wishes, but there is not much point in doing so, unless it is possible that the Inspector will need help in identifying special features of the site or its location. With the appellant attending, the LPA will probably want to send a representative along, but neither this representative nor the appellant can be permitted to address the Inspector with arguments or comments.

The Ministry lays down a strict timetable for exchange of paperwork in the written procedure and it is in the appellant's interests to adhere to it. Failure to do so may result in a delayed decision.

In the event that an informal hearing has been agreed, the applicant will be provided with a copy of a 'Code of Practice' handbook, explaining the procedure. The main requirement is for both sides to prepare their cases as for the written procedure and exchange them not later than 21 days before the hearing. The Inspector will have copies for detailed study prior to the hearing and will be able to guide the discussion along a properly objective course. There is much to commend the informal hearing procedure to the appellant who is dispensing with professional aid. A person who might be over-awed to some extent by the atmosphere of a local inquiry will find it easier to take an effective part in the proceedings and to make verbal points. It is not usual for legal representation to be employed at these hearings.

LOCAL INQUIRY

Local inquiry procedure starts in the same way as the written procedure with submission of an appeal statement 'bundle' to the Ministry, copies to the LPA, except for documents it has already seen. The Ministry will acknowledge receipt and will follow up, suggesting a date for the inquiry. The date must be acceptable to both appellant and LPA, but the rule is that only one refusal is allowed from each side. A minimum period of notice for the inquiry is six weeks, but circumstances may arise so that an earlier date can be offered. When the date is fixed there will be a formal notification, with venue and starting time, from the Ministry to the appellant, the LPA and any other parties concerned.

To facilitate a streamlined inquiry the fullest exchange of information is required beforehand. Early on, the LPA and appellant will submit pre-inquiry statements, together with all supporting plans, documents and copies of directions and opinions from other authorities and Government departments. Main evidence, known as 'Proofs of Evidence', will be exchanged 21 days before the Inquiry. The Inspector will ask for further information if he feels that either party has been too economical in the matter of providing data.

At the inquiry hearing the proceedings are a mixture of the formal and the informal. General principles for the giving of evidence and the questioning of witnesses are much the same as in a court of law, but some of the stricter rules of evidence are not observed. To open the inquiry the presiding Inspector will introduce himself and outline the terms of reference. He will note the particulars of representatives of the appellant and the LPA and will enquire as to the format of their case presentations numbers of witnesses, and so on. Then he will ask any other parties present who may wish to be heard to declare themselves and whether or not they will be calling witnesses. The Inspector is sizing up the approximate length of time needed for the inquiry and obtaining a forewarning of any interventions by other parties which may tend towards the introduction of irrelevancies to the main issue.

Unless there is some very good reason for departing from the normal sequence of an inquiry (and that is a very unusual occurrence) the appellant's case will be stated first. The appellant (or his representative) can make an opening statement, introducing and summarising the facts and arguments that will comprise the appeal. Following this, the appellant and/or other witnesses can give evidence and may be required to answer questions put by the Inspector, the LPA representative and other interested parties or their representatives.

The LPA case is presented next. The authority is usually represented by one of its officials, sometimes a planning officer, but more often than not, a solicitor from the authority's administrative staff. Witnesses called by the LPA can be questioned by the appellant or his representative and by other interested parties or their representatives, as well as by the Inspector.

When the cases for the two contesting parties have been heard, other interested parties can make their submissions and can be questioned by or on behalf of the appellant, by the LPA representative and by the Inspector.

Finally, closing statements can be made by or for the appellant and the LPA and, if the Inspector permits, by or for intervening parties. These closing statements must not attempt to introduce any new facts or arguments. They are intended to summarise and emphasise evidence already given and to point out weaknesses in other parties' evidence.

An unrepresented appellant, doing his own thing, is unlikely to have the skills of advocacy possessed by solicitors and barristers who may be appearing on behalf of the LPA and other parties intervening in the appeal and must therefore be at some disadvantage. But he will receive help from the Inspector, whose task it is to ensure that all relevant facts and arguments are brought out. It often happens that an appellant, through inexperience, omits to ask an important question which could produce an answer of considerable relevance to the appeal - and the Inspector steps in to ask that question. No appellant should be afraid to let the Inspector know that he is inexperienced in planning matters and the conduct of planning appeals and that he will be grateful for guidance when he is uncertain of procedure.

A lot depends on the attitude and personality of the Inspector in charge of an inquiry. Most Inspectors are patient (even long suffering!) men or women who bring a lot of well-judged flexibility to their control of inquiries. Occasionally one can encounter an Inspector with a stricter attitude to procedure and giving an impression of having less sympathy with inexperience. That impression may be quite false, but can nevertheless be off-putting to a nervous appellant. It isn't a good idea to allow any feeling of resentment of the attitude or rulings of an Inspector to be reflected in demeanour. Shouting, derogatory asides, interruptions and other behaviour of that sort is a bad mistake and should be avoided. It is normal practice to address the Inspector as 'Sir': you don't have to, but it certainly doesn't do any harm.

PRESENTING EVIDENCE

The usual way of giving evidence at an inquiry is to prepare in advance a written statement of what the appellant or other witness is going to say. This is called 'Proof of Evidence' and there should be sufficient copies available for the Inspector, the LPA and other parties. The copies should have been exchanged with the LPA and submitted to the Inspector 21 days before the Inquiry. A summary is read out at the Inquiry, but the witness will be examined on the evidence submitted in his Proof. Questions, as necessary, will then follow. One advantage of using proof of evidence is that there is less risk of something being forgotten or of mistakes being made in speaking from memory. It also relieves the Inspector of the need to make notes on the witness's statement. Time may be saved, too, when the proof of evidence covers a very long statement and the Inspector feels able to agree to accept it without all of it being read aloud.

When it comes to questioning witnesses, applicants acting on their own behalf often fall foul of several pitfalls besetting the inexperienced. Although rules of evidence are not as strictly applied as in a court of law, flagrant 'leading' of witnesses may arouse strong objections. Obvious attempts to put words into the mouth of a witness should not be made, even though it sometimes seems to be the only way to get the witness to say what is required and what is true. In this sort of situation the questioner may well be advised to seek the aid of the Inspector. A polite, but entreating, "Sir, I am in some difficulty here..." may produce valuable assistance.

Losing the temper or becoming over-aggressive in questioning is another serious error. It is perhaps a result of watching too many television courtroom dramas that creates a false impression of the effectiveness of snarling and shouting at witnesses. A little pardonable heat now and again may not bring a rebuke from the Inspector, but an ill-mannered exhibition will bring a swift remonstrance.

A good rule to remember is that it is the *answers* to questions that constitute the evidence. The value of the question is found in the answer it produces. The notes made by the Inspector will be of witnesses' replies. A theatrical style and oratorical tricks in the posing of questions count for nought.

After all parties have had their say the Inspector will close the inquiry. If he has not already visited the site of the development he will do so and the same conditions as those mentioned previously will apply.

All parties in an inquiry must pay their own costs. The exception to this is when an appellant or the LPA is able to show that he or they incurred unnecessary expense by the unreasonable behaviour of the other party. One of the most likely forms of unreasonable behaviour is causing postponements or adjournments by creating situations which were deliberate or easily avoidable. The Minister of State or the Inspector is empowered to make orders for the payment by the offender of the whole or part of the other party's costs.

DECISION

The eventual decision on the appeal will be communicated in a letter to the appellant from the Secretary of State or the Inspector, depending on who is authorised to make the decision, and copied to the LPA and other concerned parties. Just as with a planning appeal to the LPA, a decision will not necessarily be a plain yes or no to the appeal. There may be partial acceptance of the appeal and special conditions or time restrictions could be required. From either side's point of view it may be a curate's egg decision.

It is likely to be several weeks before the decision is given, but in some cases the Inspector may be willing to provide an early warning within a matter of only days in the form of an Advance Notice of Decision, indicating the sort of decision which can be expected. But this will be merely a 'tip-off', as it were. Only the formal notification of decision, following some time later, can be taken as the official decision.

A decision from the Secretary of State's office will quote the report and recommendations of the Inspector and will nearly always confirm the recommended decision. However, it does sometimes happen that the Minister will override the Inspector's verdict. There have been occasions when, for example, the well-founded objections to a development by the LPA have been upheld by the Inspector in recommending rejection of the developer's appeal, but the Minister has reversed the Inspector's decision. Such ministerial overturning of decisions are accompanied by a statement of reasons.

Occasionally it appears that an Inspector's recommendation, although based on valid considerations of planning control, is adjudged to be in conflict with or out of sympathy with some aspect of Government policy at that time. A Ministerial intention to reject an Inspector's recommendation is notified to the appellant and the LPA beforehand, so that both sides can comment before the formal decision notification. One possible result is a re-opening of the inquiry, but that is very much a rarity.

There is no appeal against an Inspector's or Ministerial decision, as far as planning control is concerned. Questions of the legality of appeal proceedings (in such things as non-compliance with official requirements) by the Ministry or the Inspector can be taken to the High Court. While a successful court action can in no way alter an appeal decision, it might force the Minister to have the appeal reconsidered.

Complaints relative to procedure can also be referred to the Council on Tribunals in London and complaints of maladministration will be investigated by the Parliamentary Ombudsman. It is unlikely that any of these post-decision actions will produce any advantage to the disappointed appellant, other than a sense of having struck a blow for justice.

THIRD PARTY INVENTION
Like the appellant and the LPA, third parties wishing to intervene in an appeal where the written procedure is used must make their arguments in writing, with such documentary support as they have available. The final date for submission to the Ministry will be made known when the appeal is formally notified by the Ministry and/or the LPA. With a local inquiry, a third party can make its intervention at almost any stage of the appeal. A written submission can be sent off direct to the Ministry or the LPA for onward transmission to the Inspector at any time prior to the opening of the inquiry. To intervene personally in the inquiry it is necessary to attend the opening of the proceedings, so that the Inspector can be informed of the wish to be heard, as explained earlier. The extent to which a third party can participate (in such things as questioning other parties' witnesses) is a matter for the Inspector to decide.

Anyone who is intervening or representing some one else

in an intervention is advised to be present throughout and to take careful note of the evidence given and the questions asked. Few things are more likely to annoy the Inspector and other principal participants in the inquiry than a third party wasting time by asking questions that have already been asked and making points that have been previously hammered home by somebody else. If you are intervening, make sure your contribution is not merely a repeat performance, that it is clearly stated without unnecessary verbiage and that it is relevant.

Third parties normally receive copies of the eventual decision, provided they have given the Inspector an address for receiving communications.

As far as an informal hearing is concerned, third parties can only act as they would with a written procedure. They cannot attend the hearing, but their written contributions will have been studied by the Inspector and taken into account as merited.

The different types of public enquiry are often designated by the relevant section numbers of the Town & Country Planning Act. Thus -

Sec. 77: concerning a planning action that has been 'called in', *i.e.* the Secretary of State has taken over decision responsibility from the local authority.

Sec. 78: hearing an appeal against a local authority decision on a planning matter.

Sec. 174: hearing an appeal against an enforcement notice.

ENFORCEMENT

Most breaches of planning regulations by private householders occur because of ignorance of what is required, but some of them are by determined recalcitrants who believe the only real sin is to be found out. They usually are! However, in the matter of enforcement of planning control the attitude of the LPA is governed, not so much by considerations of whether the offender is innocently ignorant or knowledgeably wilful, as by the seriousness of the breach. The power of an LPA to take specific enforcement action is discretionary.

LPAs have enforcement officers on their staffs to carry out surveillance and contact work associated with enforcement of planning control. They do not have to be qualified planning officers, although they will have been trained in planning concepts and procedures.

For the wayward developer the arrival on his doorstep of one of these officers is usually the first indication that he may be at odds with the planning authority. The object of the visit will be to confirm the facts, acquaint the developer with the situation and, if possible at that time, inform him of the action he needs to take.

The types of situation involving a private house holder and causing a visit from the enforcement officer are these

i) A change of use (in planning terms) has occurred. For example, the householder is carrying on some kind of business activity in part of the premises.

ii) A development for which planning permission is required has taken place or has been started, but no planning application has been submitted.

iii) As for ii) above, except that, although a planning application has been put in, no decision has yet been given.

iv) A planning application for change of use or some other development has been rejected, but the applicant has continued with the development in spite of the LPA decision.

v) The LPA has approved a planning application subject to certain conditions or limitations, but the developer has continued without observance of these restrictions.

It will be the aim of the LPA to get things put right with as little delay and fuss as possible. It is empowered to serve enforcement notices on offending developers, although it does not have to take such action, as such powers are discretionary. If the developer accepts what is put forward by the LPA as necessary corrective action and gives a firm commitment to implement that action without unnecessary delay, the LPA will probably take no further action - unless the developer reneges. In situations i) and ii) the LPA may well request that a planning application is made as quickly as possible to regularise matters. Such a request is often - but not necessarily - an indication that the application will be approved. With situation iii) the developer will probably be told that the development must be held in abeyance pending a decision on the application. In iv) and v) the developer will certainly be warned of the possible consequences of ignoring a planning authority decision and the LPA may endeavour to secure compliance. A change in the development, giving a better chance of approval, may be suggested.

Breach of planning control is not a criminal offence, but injunctions may be taken out to restrain actual or suspected breaches of control. However, the display of unauthorised advertisements, unauthorised works to listed buildings and unauthorised works to preserved trees are criminal offenses.

The LPA may serve a Planning Contravention Notice [PCN], which is a means of gathering information when it is suspected that a breach of control may have occurred. The types of information asked for cover the activities carried on, when they began, the names and addresses of those carrying them out or having an interest in the land, and why permission was not thought to have been required. Failure to respond to a PCN or supplying false information attracts a heavy fine.

The LPA may serve a Breach of Condition Notice [BCN], where there is a clear breach of a condition attached to a planning permission, *e.g.* exceeding stipulated operating hours.

ENFORCEMENT NOTICE
In any situation regarded by the LPA as quite unacceptable within the scope of planning control or as being immediately detrimental to the local environment, it may at once proceed with serving an enforcement notice. It may also do so when earlier efforts to persuade a developer to meet requirements have been abortive. An enforcement notice is - short of action in the courts - in the nature of a last resort on the part of the

LPA and should be taken very seriously by the recipient. It can be served on the owner, the occupier or any other person who the LPA considers has an interest in the land.

The contents of an enforcement notice are
a) particulars of the breach of planning regulations alleged by the LPA;
b) the action which the LPA requires to be taken to rectify the breach (and this may include such things as demolishing structures and taking other steps to restore land or buildings to their pre-development state);
c) the time limits imposed by the LPA for compliance with the requirements cited in the notice.

The LPA must send copies of the notice to owners and/or occupiers of the land (where they exist in addition to the developer) and to any other persons whose interest in the land could be materially affected by the proposed development. These copies must be served within 28 days of the date of issue of the notice and at least 28 days before the date on which the notice takes effect.

Enforcement action can only be taken by the LPA before the expiry of four years in the case of conversions to dwellings and ten years in the case of changes of use. The four year rule does not apply to listed buildings. Compliance with an enforcement notice does not discharge the notice; it remains a charge on the land and may be re-activated should the breach re-occur. It cannot, however, be used should a different breach occur, when the whole procedure starts again!

Anyone receiving an enforcement notice has four options. He can procure the quickest possible end to the matter by complying with the LPA's requirements. He can seek some sort of compromise arrangement that will be acceptable to the LPA, while going a bit nearer to his original development aims. He can appeal against the notice. Or he can simply ignore the notice!

Complete disregard of the notice is inviting the authority to implement the next stage of its enforcement powers, which is to prosecute in the courts. Mere disagreement with an LPA decision is unlikely to be an effective defence and it is difficult to see how any one could derive any sort of advantage from being taken to court in those circumstances. Failure to comply with an enforcement notice is a criminal offence for which the penalty is £20,000 on summary conviction, and an unlimited fine on indictment. The LPA also has powers to undertake works to ensure compliance and to charge the perpetrator the costs. So, leaving aside this lemming-style option, consider the alternatives.

An immediate response to the enforcement notice could be a sensible preliminary to any one of them, which is to have a further talk with the LPA, an exploratory discussion aimed at probing the possibility of a compromise solution and, in any event, making quite sure that the reasoning behind the LPA's attitude is understood completely. If there is no chance of compromise the choice between full compliance with the notice and an appeal against the notice must be made and can only be made on the basis of clear understanding of the case against the development. If an appeal is lodged it has the effect of putting the requirement of the notice on hold until the appeal has been determined. Note, however, that it is the appellants' duty to demonstrate that the alleged breaches have not occurred.

Obviously, there will be much benefit from professional advice - from a planning consultant or perhaps a solicitor specialising in planning matters. But the strength of the advice can best be evaluated from one's own careful appraisal of the situation.

APPEALS AGAINST ENFORCEMENT NOTICES

Pursuance of the right to appeal to the Ministry follows much the same lines as those for appeal against planning application decisions. The appeal will be determined either by the Secretary of State or by his appointed Inspector. The LPA should send an appeal form with the enforcement notice.

Strictly speaking, it is not essential to use the form for stating the grounds of appeal - a letter can be used instead - but the form is preferable since it acts as a sort of check list for the vital ingredients of the appeal statement.

Possible grounds for appeal are
i) Planning permission should be given for the development in question (or, if qualified permission was given subject to certain conditions, that these conditions be set aside).
ii) That the matters have not occurred.
iii) That the matters, if they have occurred, are not a breach of

planning control.

iv) The development complained of took place more than four years or ten years before the date of the enforcement notice.

v) The Enforcement Notice was not properly served on some of the people entitled to receive a copy.

vi) Action required by the notice exceeds what is necessary for correction of the breach or not enough time is allowed for remedial action to be carried out.

Obviously, the grounds of appeal must be relevant to the reasons given by the LPA for issuing the enforcement notice and will have to be supported by evidence of fact. The grounds as in i) are in effect an application for a planning permission decision by the Ministry and should be supported by the same sort of evidence that would go with a normal planning application. In ii) and iii) it will probably be a matter of arguing planning regulation interpretation. With iv) it is necessary to be specific on dates and to provide names and particulars of other people who were concerned earlier with the development. In some instances it may be feasible to show that a change of use (other than to a single dwelling house) or other breach happened in the first instance more than ten years before the notice was served and has been continued uninterrupted since then. The procedural grounds v) must be backed by positive assurances from the persons concerned. An appeal based on vi) requires support from solid facts and will be more credible if accompanied by arguable counter-proposals to the required activity and timing.

Proper attention to timetable observance is important in the appeal procedure. The appeal form or statement has to be in the hands of the Ministry before the date on which the notice becomes effective. It isn't advisable to do things in a rush at the last moment. The appeal documents should be sent by recorded delivery and first class mail at the earliest possible time and not later than a clear week before the final date.

Unauthorised alterations to listed buildings can be controlled through listed building enforcement notices, as can unauthorised demolition and demolition of unlisted buildings in Conservation Areas. Should the case proceed to Crown Court penalties can be very heavy indeed.

The removal or lopping of a tree which is the subject of a Tree Preservation Order without consent is a criminal offence, carrying a heavy fine and entailing the replacement of the tree. A protected tree which is dangerous or dying may be removed or lopped without consent, although a replacement tree will probably be required if the tree has been removed.

A fee is payable and must go with the appeal papers. The scale of fees is similar to that used for planning applications, but details will have been supplied with the appeal form. An appeal is exempt from fee payment if the development is the subject of a planning application on which the LPA has not given a decision before the date of the enforcement notice and where the correct fee has been paid for with the application. Exemption may also apply where the development is concerned with the provision of additional facility or comfort for a disabled person. If there is some doubt as to the amount of the fee, the appeal papers can be sent in without payment, but should be accompanied by a letter explaining why the fee is withheld and promising that it will be forwarded immediately the correct amount is known.

The Ministry will acknowledge receipt of the appeal and may request more information or clarification of information given. It is usual for a 28 day time limit to be set for making a response to this request.

As with appeals against planning application decisions, the Ministry can decide that, for reasons of public interest or complexity of evidence, the appeal should be determined by local inquiry, the decision to be given either by the Minister or by an inspector appointed by him. But the probability is that the appeal will be dealt with on the basis of the written evidence submitted. Whichever procedure is chosen it will be similar to the equivalent procedure in a planning application appeal, as outlined in the previous chapter.

Appendix

WHERE TO FIND INFORMATION, ADVICE, HELP

MINISTERIAL ADDRESSES:
Department of the Environment, 2 Marsham Street, London, SWIP 3EB. Tel. 0171-276 0900.
The Welsh Office, Cathays Park, Cardiff, CF1 3NQ. Tel. 01222 825111
Planning Inspectorate, Department of Environment & Transport, Tollgate House, Houlton Street, Bristol, BS2 9DJ. *Appeal forms (for England) are obtained from the Inspectorate. For Wales, apply to the Welsh Office.*

PROFESSIONAL ASSISTANCE:
Royal Town Planning Institute, 26 Portland Place, London WIN 4BE. Tel. 0171-636 9107. *Will provide a free brochure titled Where to find planning advice, listing the chartered planning consultants in your region.*
Royal Institute of British Architects, 66 Portland Place, London WIN 4AD. Tel. 0171-580 5533. *Advice on appointment of an architect.*
Royal Institution of Chartered Surveyors, 12 Great George Street, London, SWIP 3AE. Tel. 0171-222 7000. *Advice on appointment of a chartered surveyor.*

VOLUNTARY ADVICE:
National Association of Citizens' Advice Bureaux, 115-123 Pentonville Road, London N1 9LZ. Tel. 0171-833 2181. *General information on services obtainable from bureaux; location of nearest bureau.*
Residents/Ratepayers Associations; Civic Interest Groups May be able to advise or assist. Your local reference library or the information office of your local government authority should be able to give you contact addresses/phone numbers.
Councillors May hold 'surgeries' on a regular basis. Enquire from your local public library, stating which Council ward you live in.

ADVICE FOR OBJECTORS:
Objectors to planning applications with conservation implications may get advice or information from the following organisations, where appropriate:
Council for Environmental Conservation, 80 York Way, London NI 9AG. Tel. 0171-278 4736.
Council for the Protection of Rural England, 25 Buckingham Palace Road, London SW1W 0PP. Tel. 0171-976 6433.
Council for the Protection of Rural Wales, 31 High Street, Welshpool, Powys SY21 7JP. Tel. 01938 2525.
Friends of the Earth, 26 Underwood Street, London N1 7JT. Tel. 0171-490 1555.
Green Belt Council for Greater London, 52 Sharps Lane, Ruislip, Middlesex HA4 7JQ. Tel. 018956 34121.
Pedestrians Association and Ramblers Association, 1-5 Wandsworth Road, London SW8 2LN. Tel. 0171-735 3270.
A *directory of voluntary groups can be obtained from:* **The National Council for Voluntary Organisations**, Regent's Wharf, All Saints Street, London N1 9RL. Tel. 0171-713 6161.

PUBLICATIONS:
Several free booklets on aspects of planning, published by the Department of the Environment, the Welsh Office and other government departments are available. Your LPA office will probably have them; if not, apply to the Department of the Environment or the Welsh Office. A *Guide to Planning Appeals* with details of procedures can be had from the Planning Inspectorate or the Planning Department of the Welsh office.
Copies of Statutes and Development orders relevant to town and country planning may be purchased from HM Stationery Office (from any HMSO bookshop or by post from HMSO, P O Box 276, London SW8 5DT - telephone enquiries to 0171-873 0011).

THE OMBUDSMEN:
The Parliamentary Commissioner for Administration (The 'Parliamentary Ombudsman'), Church House, Great Smith Street, London SWIP 3BL. Tel. 0171-276 3000. The Parliamentary Ombudsman is authorised to investigate people's claims to have sustained injustice in consequence of maladministration in Government departments and in a number of other public bodies. This would include complaints in connection with the handling of planning matters by the Department of the Environment (or other ministry). Initially the complaint must be submitted to a Member of Parliament (not necessarily the MP for the complainant's constituency). The MP may decide that the matter can be pursued effectively through other official channels.
The Commission for Local Administration (The 'Local Ombudsman') [in England] 21 Queen Anne's Gate, London SWIH 9BU. Tel. 0171-222 5622. [in Wales] Derwen House, Court Road, Bridgend, Glamorgan CF3 1BN. Tel. 0656 61325. [in Scotland] 5 Shandwick Place, Edinburgh EH2 4RG. Tel. 031-229 4472. Local Ombudsmen are concerned with complaints of maladministration in local government (including local planning authorities). The initial approach must be through an elected member of the local authority.
Council on Tribunals, 22 Kingsway, London WC2. Tel. 0171-936 7045. *Investigates complaints of wrong procedures in dealing with planning appeals.*

Advance Notice of Decision 42
Advertising signs 13
Aerials 11
Agricultural tenants 24,37
Appeal procedures 35
Appeals 3,33,48,50
Application fees 24
Areas of Outstanding Natural
 Beauty 3,9,10
Article 4 4,8
Aviaries 10
Bed-sitters 16
Block plan 19
Boats 13
Breach of Condition Notice 46
Building plans 19
Building sites 7
Bulk oil storage 11
Business use 13,15,31
Caravans 13
Certificate of Lawful Use 20
Change of use 13,15,31,45,47
Citizens' Advice Bureaux 34,51
Civic societies 8,29,51
Commercial delivery vans 13
Conservation areas 3,8,9,10,11,
 12,13,14,49
Conservatories 10
Costs 42
Councillors 29,51
Covenants 4,7,8,13
Decisions 26,42
Decoration *see* Exterior decoration
Demolition 7,14
Development defined 1
Development plan 4
Dish-shaped aerials 11
Dog kennels 10
Driveways 12
Enforcement 32,45
Enforcement notices 45
Employment bureaux 16
Established use 49
Evidence presentation 41
Existing planning consent 5,7
External storage tanks 11
Extensions 8
Exterior decoration 5,8
Fees 24,50
Fences 12
Flagpoles 11
Flats 8,16

Fly-posting 13
Footways 12
Formal objections 29
Forms 21
Full planning permission 20
Garages 10,17
Garden development 5
Garden sheds 10
Garden space 8,10
Gateways 3
Granny annexes 9
Green Belt 3
Greenhouses 10
Hard standing 12,13
Hedges 12
Height of roof 9
Highway 7
Hire cars 13
Infilling 8
Informing owners 23,47
Land Register 5
Letters of objection 30
Limited permission 45
List Building Consent 21
Listed Buildings 3,8,9,12,14,47,
 49
Loading & unloading 16
Local development plans 4
Local Inquiry 35,38
Local Ombudsman 53
Location plans
Lodgers 16
Loft conversions 8,9
National Parks 3,9,10
New premises 7
Norfolk Broads 9
Objections 28
Obstruction 16
Offices 13
Oil storage tanks 11
Ombudsmen 53
Outbuildings 4,10
Outlets 7
Outline application 19
Ownership 47
Parliamentary Ombudsman 53
Parking space 5
Pathways 12
Paying guests 16
Petitions 30
Planning Application 2,18,45
Planning Contravention Notice 46

Planning control 1,8
Planning Inspectorate 51
Planning objection 2
Planning permission 7
Plans & drawings 18
Porches 10
Posters 13
Poultry pens 10
Presentation of evidence 41
Proof of evidence 41
Prospective purchaser 18
Publications 52
Radio Aerials 11
Rainwater catchment tanks 11
Renewal of limited permission 20
Repairs & decorations 8
Reserved matters 20
Residents' Associations 8,29,34, 51
Restricted use 4
Roofs 11
Rooftop aerials 11
Safety hazards 7
Satellite dishes 11
Self-contained flats 16
Sheds 10
Signs 13

Site inspection 42
Site plan 18
Sites of Special Scientific Interest 3
Solar panels 14
Storage 13,17,31
Storage tanks 11
Summer houses 10
Sun lounges 10
Swimming pools 10
Taxicabs 13
Tenants' Associations 29
Third party Intervention 43
Town & Country Planning Act 1, 14
Trade vehicles 13,17
Tree Preservation Orders 14,49
Trees 14
Types of planning application 19
Vehicle outlet 7
Vehicle repair 31
Verandahs 10
View on vehicle highway
Walls 3,12
Water storage tanks 11
Written procedure 35,37